Johannes Kepler

Exploring the Mysteries of God's Universe

Michael Stamp & Christy Hardy

Dallas, Texas
ICR.org

Johannes Kepler
Exploring the Mysteries of God's Universe
by Michael Stamp and Christy Hardy

First printing: March 2022

Copyright © 2022 Institute for Creation Research. All rights reserved. No portion of this book may be used in any form without written permission of the publisher, with the exception of brief excerpts in articles and reviews. For more information, write to Institute for Creation Research, P. O. Box 59029, Dallas, TX 75229.

Series concept and direction: Jayme Durant, ICR Director of Communications
Senior Editor: Beth Mull
Editors: Lori Fausak and Truett Billups
Graphic Designer and Illustrator: Susan Windsor

All Scripture quotations are from the New King James Version.

ISBN: 978-1-946246-77-6
Library of Congress Control Number: 2022933951

Please visit our website for other books and resources: ICR.org

Printed in the United States of America.

Table of Contents

Foreword 5

Introduction 7

Chapter 1: Searching the Skies 10

Chapter 2: The Mystery of the Universe 23

Chapter 3: Groundbreaking Discoveries 29

Chapter 4: New Ideas 37

Chapter 5: Marriage, Family, and Tragedy .. 43

Chapter 6: Kepler's Laws 46

Chapter 7: Finishing Strong 51

Endnotes 61

Timeline 62

Glossary 63

"We see how God, like a human architect, approached the founding of the world according to order and rule and measured everything in such a manner."[1]

— Johannes Kepler

Foreword

Johannes Kepler is featured here in the Heroes of Creation Science series because he believed God created the universe and would help him uncover its mysteries through science. His Christian faith helped him endure incredible hardship and loss to become one of the great founders of modern astronomy.

Did you know the Bible credits the Lord Jesus Christ as the Creator who formed all of the heavenly bodies? Hebrews 1:1-2 tells us that God has spoken to us by His Son, "through whom also He made the worlds." In that same chapter, God says to Jesus, "You, Lord, in the beginning laid the foundation of the earth, and the heavens are the work of Your hands."

So when you read about the amazing things Kepler discovered in the universe, you can remember that Jesus created it all!

Johannes Kepler 1571–1630

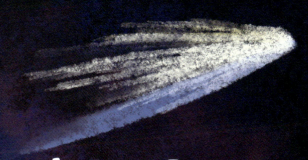

Introduction

Johannes Kepler was a founder of modern astronomy and possibly one of the greatest scientists who ever lived. He began studying the planets and stars before the telescope was even invented!

Kepler was a mathematician and astronomer during the Scientific Revolution of the 17th century, a time when several key discoveries changed the way people saw the world around them.

Revolutions in learning can open people's minds to new and better ideas. As scientists share discoveries with each other, one's work builds on the progress of another's.

Kepler learned from astronomers like Nicolaus Copernicus and Tycho Brahe, who carefully studied and mapped the planets and stars. And scientists like Isaac Newton built on Kepler's work.

The Scientific Revolution overlapped a difficult time in Europe known as the Reformation, a period when Protestants split from the Roman Catholic Church. For many years Kepler was caught in the middle of this struggle, and this influenced his entire

Nicolaus Copernicus and Tycho Brahe

life. He was a Protestant whose writings reflect his deep faith in God's grace and guidance. People tried to force Kepler to deny his faith, but he would not.

Kepler held tightly to his Christian convictions even as he endured persecution. He believed God

Page from the Gutenberg Bible, which was part of the printing revolution that contributed to the Reformation

would help him uncover the architecture of the universe, and this inspired his scientific efforts. Let's go back in time about 400 years and look at the incredible impact of Johannes Kepler's life.

Chapter 1
Searching the Skies

Johannes Kepler was born near the city of Stuttgart in southern Germany in 1571. He did not have an easy childhood. At the time, Germany was part of the Holy Roman Empire. His family had little money. His

The Great Comet of 1577 was seen all around the world and was studied by astronomers in many countries.

father, a professional soldier, left the family when Kepler was only five years old. He never returned. And that wasn't Kepler's only challenge. About that same time he contracted smallpox, which damaged his vision and crippled his hands.

At the age of six, Kepler's mother took him to a "high place" to see the Great Comet of 1577 blaze through the night sky. All of Europe was excited to see such a bright wonder in the heavens. When he was nine, Kepler also witnessed the moon turn red during a lunar eclipse. Seeing these incredible events drew Kepler's curiosity to the heavens and sparked his keen interest in astronomy. This, combined with his excellent math skills, fueled his many accomplishments later in life.

> ### *Eclipse*
> Lunar *eclipses* occur when Earth orbits between the sun and the moon. This temporarily casts Earth's shadow on the moon. It also causes the moon to appear red because the sun's rays are filtered as they travel through Earth's atmosphere.

Encountering New Ideas

After grammar school, Kepler attended the University of Tübingen. His plan was to study theology, become a Protestant pastor, and spread the gospel of faith in Jesus Christ. From 1591 to 1594 Kepler studied theology (study of God), along with philosophy (study of knowledge, values, right and wrong, etc.) and math. When astronomer and math professor Michael Maestlin introduced Kepler to Nicolaus Copernicus' new ideas about the solar system, it changed the course of Kepler's life.

Copernicus' ideas are widely accepted today, but they were unpopular in Kepler's time. Many people believed the Bible teaches that Earth is the center of the universe, an idea known as the geocentric model. So they thought Copernicus' idea of a heliocentric (sun-centered) universe had to be wrong. But Kepler didn't see the heliocentric model as a threat to the Scriptures. He saw it as a beautiful, orderly reflection of God's design.

Michael Maestlin

Considering Copernicus

Kepler still dearly wanted to be a Lutheran Christian minister. But at age 22 he was recruited to be a mathematics and

Did you know?

In verses like Ecclesiastes 1:5, the Bible talks about the sun "rising" or "going down." But Copernicus' sun-centered model showed the sun as staying in one place. Kepler did not see this as a problem because the Scriptures are describing the sun's appearance from a human perspective. Today, people still talk about the sun "rising" and "setting" even though we know for certain that Earth's rotation causes sunrises and sunsets.

astronomy teacher at a Protestant school in Graz, Germany. When he arrived in 1594, not many students attended his classes. In fact, he had to take on a second job as a calendar maker just to make ends meet.

In 1543 Nicolaus Copernicus published his theory that Earth orbits the sun.

Thankfully, this gave Kepler more time to consider Copernicus' heliocentric model of the solar system, and he wondered what held the sun, Earth, and the other planets in place. He concluded that some force of the sun must be keeping the planets moving in their orbits. Since gravity was an unknown concept at the time, he thought some kind of magnetic force must be the

Copernicus' heliocentric model of the solar system

key. And he hoped this would explain why Mars sometimes appears to move backwards (called retrograde motion). Not even Copernicus' model could explain it.

Kepler's ideas didn't always turn out to be right, but he remained determined to prove that Copernicus' heliocentric model was accurate.

A page from Copernicus' book on heliocentrism

"I wanted to become a theologian. For a long time I was restless. Now, however, behold how through my effort God is being celebrated in astronomy."

— Johannes Kepler's letter to Michael Maestlin, October 3, 1595

What Was the Reformation?

Martin Luther was a pastor and leader of a religious movement known as the Reformation. He pointed out unbiblical beliefs that had been adopted by the Roman Catholic Church. Those who followed Luther's teachings formed Protestant churches.

Protestants were known for their belief in the free gift of salvation that anyone can receive through faith in Jesus Christ. Faith

Statue of Martin Luther (1483–1546)

> For by grace you have
> been saved through faith,
> and that not of yourselves;
> it is the gift of God.
> (Ephesians 2:8)

alone, not by works, as it says in Scripture.

Luther wanted the Word of God in the hands of regular people so they could read it for themselves. Many had never read a Bible because Bibles were written in Latin. So more people could understand God's Word, Luther translated the Bible into the common German language. With the help of the newly invented printing press, these Bibles quickly spread throughout Europe. Johannes Kepler was born on the heels of this movement, and it influenced his life, his faith, and even his scientific pursuits.

The Copernican Revolution

Nicolaus Copernicus (1473–1543) was a Polish astronomer. His heliocentric model of the solar system places the sun in the center with the planets orbiting around it. Before Copernicus came along, most scientists believed the sun and the planets orbit Earth. They used the geocentric (Earth-centered) model developed by Greek astronomer Claudius Ptolemy hundreds of years earlier.

Scientists believed the geocentric model to be true for over 1,300 years, but they had it backwards! We now know Earth, the other planets, asteroids, and comets all orbit the sun.

It might look like the sun orbits Earth when we see it rise in the east and set in the west each day, but that's because Earth is always spinning on its axis.

It's the job of scientists to stay curious and seek the true nature of things, because things are not always as they first appear. Scientists must keep questioning and studying even when issues seem to be settled.

Comets

Like Earth and the other planets, comets in our solar system orbit the sun. Comet orbits are extremely elliptical. These icy bodies lose water and dust when they travel close to the sun. As the comet vaporizes, a beautiful tail streams from it. If comets were billions of years old, they would have already melted away. Some scientists think old comets are replaced with new ones, but no one has seen this happen. Comets are evidence that our solar system was created recently.

C/2020 F3, Comet NEOWISE

Elliptical

An *ellipse* is a squashed circle. An *elliptical* orbit comes in close to the sun, loops around far away, and then comes close again.

When NASA's Deep Impact *space probe flew by Comet Hartley 2 in 2010, scientists were surprised to find it was spitting out carbon dioxide. Since it would have no gas left after billions of years, it has to be a lot younger—like thousands of years old.*

> ## Did you know?
> The Great Comet of 1577 is a non-periodic comet, which means it won't return for a very long time—if ever.

Chapter 2
The Mystery of the Universe

One particular day, July 19, 1595, Kepler felt that God revealed to him a mystery of the universe through his studies. Kepler saw the planets' order and balance and believed he'd discovered God's architecture for the solar system.

In 1596 he published his first work, *Mysterium Cosmographicum*, which means "the

An image from Mysterium Cosmographicum

mystery of the universe." In it he defended Copernicus' sun-centered model using math and geometry. A series of three-dimensional shapes called platonic solids appeared to explain the orbits and distances between the known planets. This theory looked right at first, and Kepler tried to prove it for years. But actually, platonic solids do not explain how the planets move around the sun.

Facing Persecution

When other astronomers read *Mysterium Cosmographicum*, word spread that Kepler was a skilled mathematician and first-rate

Persecution

Poor treatment, threats, or even violence toward a person or group of people because of their country of origin, appearance, or beliefs

Barbara Müller and Johannes Kepler

astronomer. He had big plans to publish more books about his research on the planets' motions in our solar system. But the persecution he faced for practicing his Protestant faith made it difficult for him to stay in Graz. During that time, he married a widow named Barbara Müller. She was 23, and he was 26. They wrote letters to each other in code so the content of their messages wouldn't stir up more persecution. Together they had five children, although two died as babies.

In 1600, Protestants in Graz were required to convert to Catholicism or leave the area.

Kepler needed to move his family to another city in order to continue his work.

At the Castle with Tycho Brahe

Kepler kept up his astronomy work and communication with other well-known scientists. One of these was the Holy Roman Emperor's chief astronomer, Tycho Brahe. In 1600 Brahe invited Kepler to work with him at the castle and observatory in Prague, the capital of today's Czech Republic.

Tycho Brahe

Brahe had compiled an enormous amount of planet and star data using only his eyes. He observed planets and more than a thousand stars before the telescope had even been invented!

Kepler's time with Brahe

> ### Did you know?
> As a student, Tycho Brahe lost part of his nose in a sword fight. To cover the scar, he wore a fake nose made of metal for the rest of his life.

didn't go as he expected. Kepler wanted to use Brahe's planetary observations to solve mysteries of the solar system. But Brahe was hesitant to share the information he had collected. However, Brahe unexpectedly died at the age of 55. On his deathbed, Brahe asked Kepler to continue his work and publish his detailed astronomical observations.

Kepler took Brahe's position as astronomer under Emperor Rudolf II. He now had access to Brahe's remarkably detailed observations. Since Kepler's eyesight was poor due to his childhood illness, he used these records in his research. It was as if Kepler was able to look at the skies through Tycho Brahe's eyes.

Kepler Wrongly Accused

In 1901, long after Kepler's death, scientists speculated that he might have poisoned Brahe in order to get access to his astronomical records. They claimed they found mercury, a toxic metal, in Brahe's remains. Thankfully, in 2010 tests showed that the amount of mercury would not have been enough to kill Brahe and had probably accumulated before he began working with Kepler. Kepler's good name and reputation were restored.

The famous Prague astronomical clock was first installed in 1410. It's the oldest known clock still operating.

Chapter 3
Groundbreaking Discoveries

In Prague, Emperor Rudolf II allowed Kepler to freely practice his Protestant faith without fear of persecution. This let Kepler focus on his work, which progressed rapidly as his mind buzzed with new ideas. He spent most of 1603 studying eyesight and the behavior of light—what scientists call optics.

Through studying the path of light through the eye, he was among the first to discover that the human eye sends the images it receives to the brain upside down. The brain then turns the images right side up. This knowledge helped people produce better eyeglasses.

In 1604, Kepler published *Astronomiae Pars Optica* (*The Optical Part of Astronomy*), a work considered to be the foundation of modern optics.

In his book Astronomiae Pars Optica, *Kepler was the first to...*

- investigate the formation of pictures with a pinhole camera
- explain the process of vision by refraction within the eye
- customize eyeglass design for nearsightedness and farsightedness
- explain the use of both eyes for depth perception

"It may be well to wait a century for a reader, as God has waited six thousand years for an observer."
— Johannes Kepler

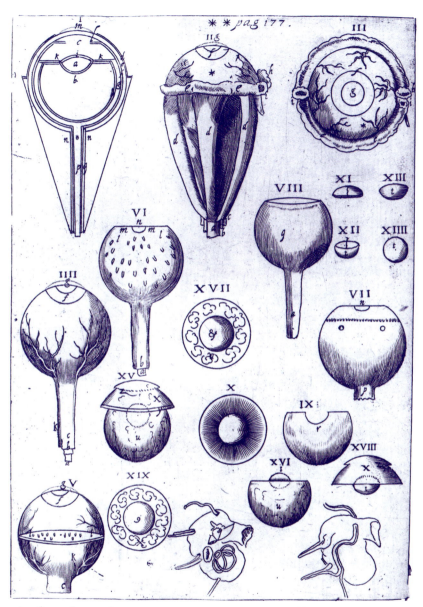

A plate from Astronomiae Pars Optica *illustrating the structure of eyes of various species*

Frosty Findings

During a snowstorm one winter, curious Kepler observed a snowflake that had fallen on his coat. Being nearsighted, he could see the tiny ice crystal clearly. Why did each snowflake have six sides? Why were no two snowflakes alike?

Kepler wrote about his frosty findings in a book called *Strena Seu de Nive Sexangular* (*A New Year's Gift of Hexagonal Snow*). Much like Kepler's research on planets and optics, this work influenced future scientists.

All snowflakes have six sides. The shapes ice crystals take can be explained by the way the water particles pack together in an orderly way as they freeze.

> **Did you know?**
> As many as 200 ice crystals stick together to form a snowflake.

Galileo's Telescope

Kepler lived at the same time as Italian astronomer and mathematician Galileo Galilei. Inspired by the lenses Dutch spectacle-maker Johann Lippershey had crafted, Galileo built a refracting telescope and pointed it at the sky. One of the first things he discovered were mountains on the moon.

In 1610 Galileo told Kepler about four new objects he had observed near Jupiter with his telescope. Galileo wanted Kepler to confirm the discovery. Kepler was excited about the new telescope and realized the objects were four moons orbiting Jupiter. Just as Kepler had seen through the eyes of Tycho Brahe, he was now seeing through the telescope of Galileo!

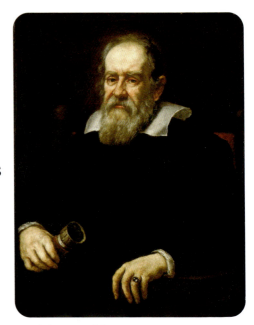

Galileo Galilei

Did you know?

In Kepler's day, telescopes weren't strong enough to clearly see the planets Uranus and Neptune or the dwarf planet Pluto. Astronomers would have to wait many years for these more distant heavenly bodies to be discovered.

Jupiter and its four moons, top to bottom: Io, Europa, Ganymede, and Callisto. They are called the Galilean moons after the man who discovered them.

How Does a Telescope Work?

Imagine the challenges faced by astronomers before they had telescopes. They were limited to what they could see with the naked eye! Galileo's telescope allowed astronomers to view distant objects, which opened up a new era of astronomy.

The telescope used two curved lenses—a large lens and a small lens—to refract (bend) light. Bending light can make faraway things appear much closer. When an astronomer points their telescope at the night sky, light from stars, planets, and moons enters the big lens. Then the small lens inside the telescope magnifies that light.

Eyeglasses also have lenses that refract light. The lenses bend light in just the right way and make faraway objects clear and sharp to a viewer who is nearsighted.

Chapter 4
New Ideas

One night, Kepler dreamed he was a boy living in Iceland who met spirits that helped humans travel great distances. In his dream, the spirits took Kepler to the moon, where he saw other strange creatures living there. Kepler wrote the novel *Somnium* based on his wild dream. Not surprisingly, the title means "The Dream" in Latin. His imaginative work described how Earth might look from the moon. Kepler's story is perhaps the first science fiction novel ever written.

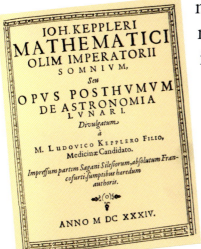

Kepler's novel Somnium. *It was written in 1608, but it wasn't published until 1634.*

> *Science Fiction*
> Stories that deal with futuristic ideas like space travel, new inventions, and life on other planets

The Star of Bethlehem

In 1614, Kepler published *De Vero Anno* (*On the Year*). In it he speculated about what astronomical event could've produced the Star of Bethlehem that guided the wise men to the house where the Christ child and his family were staying.

Now after Jesus was born in Bethlehem of Judea in the days of Herod the king, behold, wise men from the East came to Jerusalem, saying, "Where is He who has been born King of the Jews? For we have seen His star in the East and have come to worship Him" (Matthew 2:1-2).

Over the years, many people have wondered about the origin of the special star in the East. From 1604 to 1605, Kepler observed a supernova that appeared in the constellation Ophiuchus. A year before that, he saw a planetary conjunction of Jupiter

Planetary Conjunction
A rare astronomical event in which two or more planets appear close together in the sky

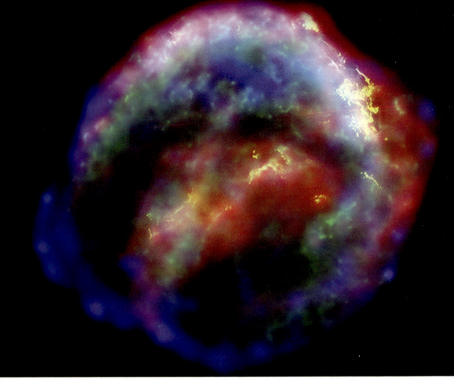

Kepler's supernova remnant

Supernova

When stars run out of fuel they eventually explode into a *supernova*, which looks like a bright, colorful cloud among the stars.

and Saturn, with Mars orbiting nearby.

According to his calculations, a similar conjunction had occurred in the year 7 BC. He wondered if this rare sight might have been the tool God used to mark Christ's birthplace for the wise men.

> *Did you know?*
> The Star of Bethlehem settled over a specific person on Earth (Matthew 2:9). So, it was probably a one-time supernatural event, not a planetary conjunction as Kepler suspected.

The Red Planet

For years Kepler studied Mars, sometimes called the Red Planet, to understand how planets move. He used many of Tycho Brahe's detailed observations in this work.

Mars didn't fit into most models of the solar system. At the time, most astronomers believed the Red Planet had a circular orbit, but Kepler used math to discover that it appeared to follow the path of an ellipse, or squashed circle.

Mars, the Red Planet

Did you know?

Unlike Mars and the other planets, Earth's orbit around the sun is almost a perfect circle. The Lord Jesus designed it that way so Earth would receive an even amount of sunlight all year long. This keeps the climate stable on Earth. It also helps make life possible because the heat coming from the sun stays the same. Earth's tilt also gives us four seasons each year.

Chapter 5
Marriage, Family, and Tragedy

The year 1611 was a tragic year for Johannes Kepler and his family. Kepler's wife, Barbara, came down with Hungarian spotted fever and died. Then all three of Kepler's children caught smallpox—the same disease he had as a child. Sadly, his son Friedrich also died.

> ### Did you know?
> In Kepler's time, medical care was quite limited. People often died of illnesses that are easily prevented or cured today. Europeans had an average life expectancy of only about 40 years. Today it's around 80 years.

The Village Doctor by David Teniers the Younger, 1636. Doctors in Kepler's day didn't have as many tools to fight disease as we do today.

With Galileo's recommendation, Kepler was offered a position as mathematics professor at the University of Padua near Venice, Italy. But Kepler wanted to keep his family in their homeland of Germany. In 1612, he left Prague and moved to Linz in western Germany to work as a math teacher.

In 1613, Kepler married again. His second

wife was Susanna Reuttinger. They had six children together, but the first three died in childhood. Even so, Kepler's marriage to Susanna was a happy one. He said that Susanna "won me over with love, humble loyalty, economy of household, diligence, and the love she gave the stepchildren."[2]

The Peasant Dance *by Pieter Brueghel the Elder, 1567*

Chapter 6
Kepler's Laws

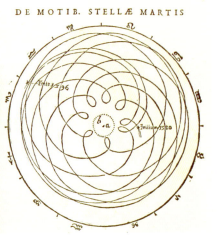

A diagram from Astronomia Nova

Kepler published *Astronomia Nova* (*The New Astronomy*) in 1609 after nearly a decade of research. In it he wrote about the first two of his three laws of planetary motion.

Studying Mars led Kepler to discover the first law. It states that all planets except Earth move in ellipses around the sun. Up until that time, most astronomers believed all the planets' orbits were perfect circles. But Kepler's careful study of Mars proved them wrong.

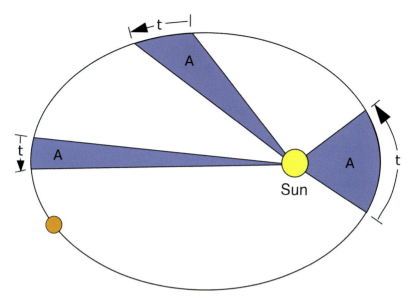

This figure illustrates Kepler's second law. If the amount of time (t) is the same, then the area covered (A) will also be the same.

Kepler's Second Law

Kepler's second law states that a planet's orbit will sweep across an equal area in a given amount of time—sometimes called the "equal areas in equal time" law. Because of the sun's gravitational pull, a planet's speed increases as its orbit nears the sun and decreases as it goes farther away. This law shows that math is a key part of astronomy and helps astronomers predict orbits today.

Kepler's Third Law

Kepler's third law was the most complex for him to discover: the time it takes a planet to orbit the sun is related to the planet's distance from the sun. Here's how it works.

The farther a planet is from the sun, the slower it moves because it's farther away from the sun's powerful gravity. Since Mercury is closest to the sun, it moves the fastest—over 107,000 miles per hour! The dwarf planet Pluto only goes about 10,000 miles per hour

Mercury

because it's so far away from the sun.

Kepler figured out this third law of planetary motion in 1618. These three laws were vital to launch the world into the era of modern astronomy. They are still used today.

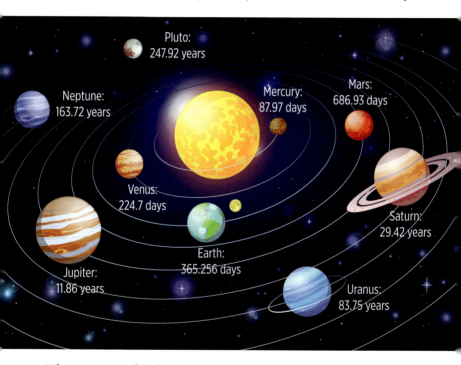

The time each planet takes to orbit the sun. Pluto lost its status as a planet in 2006 and is now called a dwarf planet.

Scientific Laws

What are scientific laws, and where do they come from?

Scientists use something called the scientific method as a logical way to look at our world. Scientists usually start with a question about something they observe in nature. Then they think of a possible answer to the question called a hypothesis—a prediction.

The scientists then test their hypothesis to see if their prediction is right. If they are able to test their hypothesis over and over and it still seems correct, the hypothesis can become a theory.

Kepler

A scientific law is a theory that's been tested and observed many, many times and has never been shown to be wrong.

Chapter 7
Finishing Strong

After publishing *Astronomia Nova* (*The New Astronomy*) in 1609, Kepler wanted to write an astronomy textbook to better explain his work. He completed the first three books of *Epitome Astronomiae Copernicanae* (*Epitome of Copernican Astronomy*) in 1615, which were then published in 1618. He ended up writing a total of seven books in this series, with the last books published in 1621.

Epitome is Kepler's most influential work. In it he explains his three laws of planetary motion in great detail. He also describes his own more precise explanations of Nicolaus Copernicus' heliocentric model of the solar system.

> *Did you know?*
> *Epitome* means brief summary or best example.

The Relief of Genoa by Antonio de Pereda shows an event that happened during the Thirty Years' War.

In 1618, the king of Bohemia, who became Holy Roman Emperor Ferdinand II in 1619, tried to impose Roman Catholicism throughout his lands. A group of Protestants revolted, and the Thirty Years' War began. This war spread to many parts of Europe, including Germany where Kepler lived. The long conflict disrupted his work. The Thirty Years' War killed millions of

Civilian
A person who isn't a soldier or police officer

people, including many civilians. But Kepler and his family survived the war.

The Rudolphine Tables

After many years of work, Kepler finally completed Tycho Brahe's lunar tables in 1623. He published them as the *Rudolphine Tables*, named after Emperor Rudolf II. Due to various challenges, including the Thirty Years' War, the tables weren't printed until 1627. At that time, these tables provided the most precise positions of the planets, the

Map from the Rudolphine Tables

moon, and stars ever produced. Over 1,000 stars were listed!

Kepler used these detailed records to test his own theories, with Mars as his main test object.

In 1631, a year after Kepler's death, astronomer Pierre Gassendi observed Mercury moving across the sun on the exact day Kepler's calculations predicted it would! Gassendi's observation showed that Kepler's hypothesis was right.

The *Rudolphine Tables* can still be used to

Statue of Johannes Kepler, 1571–1630, in Linz, Germany

accurately determine the locations of planets at any time in the past, present, or future.

Death of a Revolutionary Scientist

In 1630, at the age of 58, Johannes Kepler became very sick with a fever and died. For decades after Kepler's death, his major work, *Epitome Astronomiae Copernicanae* (*Epitome of Copernican Astronomy*), was the most widely used astronomy textbook in Europe. Just as he had hoped, it changed people's minds about how the solar system works.

Kepler didn't live to see the fruits of his labor. It took many years for other scientists to fully understand and appreciate his work. But eventually scientists came to realize that Earth does indeed orbit the sun.

Ahead of His Time

Johannes Kepler was one of the greatest mathematicians and astronomers who ever lived. He used math to better understand the movements of our planets and moons. He saw God's design in Copernicus' heliocentric model of the solar system, and he confirmed that it was accurate. He viewed the graceful balance of our solar system as God's creative architecture. He saw perfect design and balance in the planets' orbits around the sun, and he used mathematics to measure their precision.

Kepler was at the forefront of the Scientific Revolution. He discovered three laws of planetary motion, made discoveries

> "O God, I am thinking Thy thoughts after Thee."
> —Johannes Kepler

in optics and ice crystals, and developed better telescopes. He also changed the way people saw the world around them. Each new discovery he made pushed science forward. Kepler's laws are foundational to astronomy, and they are still used by astronomers today!

A talking Johannes Kepler portrait in the ICR Discovery Center in Dallas, Texas

The Kepler Space Telescope

NASA launched the Kepler space telescope in March 2009 to find out if there's life in other parts of the universe. It was named after—you guessed it—Johannes Kepler. The mission's objective was to search the Milky Way galaxy for other Earth-size planets that orbit in what is called the "habitable zone." This is the area where a planet's temperature would support liquid water, which is needed to sustain life.

For nine-and-a-half years, the Kepler space telescope studied over 530,000 stars, found 61 supernovas, and confirmed the existence of thousands of planets outside our solar system.

The spacecraft discovered that most stars

have at least one planet orbiting them—each a unique world.

The Kepler spacecraft mission ended in 2018. And guess what? The Kepler mission, and all missions like it, have never discovered life outside of Earth. Our planet is perfect for life, with its oceans, plants, atmosphere, orbiting distance from the sun, tide-making moon, and our just-right warm sun. The Lord Jesus created Earth for life and made all kinds of plants and animals to fill it…and He made Earth especially to be our home!

The fact that there are so many stars and planets out there that can't sustain life reveals to us just how special Earth is.

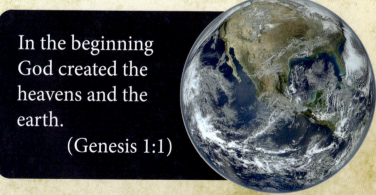

In the beginning God created the heavens and the earth.
(Genesis 1:1)

Building on Kepler's Work

Another famous scientist, Isaac Newton, studied Kepler's work, and it helped him take the next leap forward in science through his work on universal gravitation. Both Newton and Kepler were men of deep faith and saw God's design in nature.

In a letter to Robert Hooke in 1675, Newton made this famous statement: "If I have seen further it is by standing on the shoulders of giants."

This quote is often used to symbolize scientific progress in general—one generation of scientists helps the next. One of the scientific giants whose shoulders Newton stood on was Johannes Kepler.

Endnotes

1. Tiner, J. H. 1977. *Johannes Kepler: Giant of Faith and Science.* Milford, MI: Mott Media, 178.
2. Connor, J. 2004. *Kepler's Witch: An Astronomer's Discovery of Cosmic Order Amid Religious War, Political Intrigue, and the Heresy Trial of His Mother.* New York: HarperCollins Publishers, Inc., 252. Quotation translated from an October 23, 1613, letter from Kepler to an anonymous nobleman.

Timeline of Johannes Kepler's Life

1571 — Born near Stuttgart, Germany

1577 — Saw the Great Comet as a boy

1589 — Attended the University of Tubingen

1594 — Took a position as mathematics professor at Graz

1596 — Published *Mysterium Cosmographicum*

1597 — Married Barbara Müller

1600 — Tycho Brahe invited Kepler to work with him in Prague

1603 — Worked on optics

1604–1605 — Observed a supernova

1610 — Communicated with Galileo

1611 — His wife, Barbara, and son Friedrich died

1613 — Married Susanna Reuttinger

1618–1621 — Published *Epitome Astronomiae Copericanae*

1623 — Completed the *Rudolphine Tables*

1630 — Died in Regensburg, Germany, at the age of 58

Glossary

Astronomy The branch of science that studies objects and events in space.

Comet An icy solar system body that vaporizes and releases gases when passing close to the sun. These gases produce a tail.

Crystal A solid material made of highly ordered microscopic structures, often translucent (light passes through it).

Galaxy A system of millions or billions of stars held together by gravitational attraction.

Geocentric An Earth-centered model of the solar system.

Gravity All things with mass or energy are attracted to each other. On Earth, gravity gives weight to objects.

Heliocentric A sun-centered model of the solar system.

Hypothesis An educated guess or prediction based on prior knowledge and observation. A hypothesis also includes an explanation of why the prediction may be correct.

Protestantism A form of Christianity that began with the 16th-century Reformation, a movement against what its followers perceived to be errors in the Catholic Church.

Refraction The bending of light as it passes through water, vapor, or glass.

Image Credits

Aldaron (via Wikipedia): 54

BigstockPhoto: 20, 38, 49

Steve Collis (via Wikipedia): 28

Giuseppe Donatiello (via Wikipedia): 11

ICR: 35t, 57

iStockPhoto: 17

Jan Mehlich (via Wikipedia): 14

NASA: 21-22, 35b, 40-41, 48, 55, 58-59

Public Domain: 4, 6 (etching), 8-10, 13, 15-16, 23, 25-26, 31-32, 34, 37, 46-47, 50, 52-53, 60

Wellcome Images: 44

For other children's resources, go to ICR.org/store